Acknowledgments

MW01154527

Thank you, thank you, thank you!!

To Mark and Cindy Pentecost and Krista Rapa (a.k.a. our parents) for your endless support, taste testing, always believing in us and forgiving our many messes in your kitchens.

To Kyler Pentecost, Kami and Nathan Dempsey and Trenton Langkamp for your love, encouragement and enthusiasm for the yeast free lifestyle.

To Brittany Ykema, an extraordinary photographer who artistically filled these pages with scrumptious photos, believing in our mission and spending countless hours lending your expertise to complete our cookbook.

Katy & Kindsey

For Your Enjoyment!

Why Yeast Free?

There are so many fads, new diets and lifestyles to choose from. We were never those ladies that thought we would be eating so cautiously. After many health issues we both found we needed to be yeast free to eliminate feeling so terrible and ironically we started looking a lot better too. We changed so much that people started asking us what was going on and asking for help. We decided to get real crafty in the kitchen to make this journey fun and yummy too. Let us explain a little about living yeast free which is also referred to as candida free.

Candida Yeast is a type of fungus that is not good for your body. It is referred to as bad bacteria. Candida exists in every body. Even if you feel healthy, bad bacteria can affect you just by being alive and manifesting in your body. Some people will be more passionate about doing something like living yeast free because they are sick of not feeling well. Generally candida yeast won't cause a health problem unless it overgrows and outweighs the good bacteria in your body. This may happen naturally or by a stimulus such as long term birth control use, poor diet, antibiotic or other drug use or systemic diseases just to name a few. There are so many people that suffer from yeast infections and probably don't even know it. Here are some symptoms that may be caused by yeast overgrowth:

Allergies, Digestion Problems, Eczema or other skin rashes, Chronic Fatigue, Stress, Aching muscles or joints, food intolerances, unexplained nerve pain, ADHD, Endometriosis, Depression, Yeast Infections, Thrush, and many more.

There is a lot of helpful research out there on the yeast free diet, but not many cook books. We found the cookbooks that are available to be, quite frankly, boring. "Eat to Survive" seemed to be the theme. We took on a passion to provide you with flavorful, easy, family friendly recipes to incorporate yeast free living into your life. Yeast free living can be so easy and delicious.

Different Phases of Yeast Free Living

Generally there are three phases of yeast free living to get your body yeast free. There are severe cases where someone might have to do a cleanse first, but in most cases you can begin in Phase I. If you are nervous about starting something cold turkey you can start by eliminating some "bad" foods from your diet and then move in to Phase I gradually. In Phase I you are detoxing, literally killing all the bad bacteria. The reason it is so important to not cheat is because if you do cheat you are just continuing to feed the bad bacteria and your cravings will grow stronger and the bad yeast will not die. In Phase II you move in to more carbs and the Lifestyle Phase you add back in some good sugars. Phase II is just preparing you for the lifestyle Phase. You stay in this Phase as long as you need to in order to figure out quantities and types of food your body can handle. When looking for health victory you may be in Phase II for a year only adding back one good carb at a time seeing how your body responds. You will know when it is time to add another type of food or ingredient. Once you add a food back in to your life, you should continue to feel great. If its too much too soon you may get bloated, nauseous or a headache which is your body telling you not to add that food back in yet or lessen the quantity.

Further in this introduction we will provide lists of types of food you can enjoy and begin adding back to your life during the different phases. This list is not exhaustive.

Welcome to Phase I of living yeast free. As we start this journey together, we want to encourage you to not read ahead to other phases.

Stay right here on Phase I. As you can see, we say 4 weeks to 8 weeks, we did Phase I for multiple weeks. We both wanted to be sure we had it down and sometimes we can be over achievers with a competitive side!

This phase eliminates certain foods while increasing other foods that are eaten in smaller amounts and more often. Phase I is very important because during this phase the yeast is killed. If you have been eating whatever you want, when you want it, this phase will be difficult but you can do it. Let us repeat....you can do this. While dining out with friends you may run into temptation. We want you to be aware and pay close attention to the comments that your friends make after eating; "I ate too much", "I feel so sick", and "I am starting my diet tomorrow". Our point is you will notice how much better you feel by eating the right food, we promise you will get to add in a lot more food as you continue through the phases of yeast free living.

The Purpose of Phase I

Starve the yeast! Our diets typically contain too much sugar. We label readers know that sugar is everywhere, found in almost everything and is disguised by many deceiving names. The only way to safely eliminate the yeast overgrowth in your body is to starve the yeast. Yeast can only survive if it is able to eat. What does yeast eat? Sugar!

You must starve the yeast in phase I by avoiding sugars and foods that contain sugar. Consuming sugars causes blood sugar levels to spike and causes the yeast to feed and grow. You have to realize as you eat yeast free in phase I, you are killing the enemy. The enemy is yeast and sugar is its only food source. If you cheat and eat sugar, you are just feeding the enemy and prolonging the yeast free journey. Eating too much sugar can double the yeast in your body in 1 hour, so it's important to only eat the food allowed in this phase. We hope you understand how important this is as you embark on your yeast free-living journey!

Before we move on to foods you can eat, lets go over supplements.

We would highly recommend a multivitamin, gentle colon cleanser with fiber, greens and probiotic. During this phase you want to make sure you are getting all the nutrients you need so you can properly detoxify body. We have found many supplements on the market use mediocre or unnatural ingredients, which don't help the body. Look for natural products made with natural whole food nutrition.

Organic is a hot topic. To get a full detox we recommend always choosing organic meat. We understand that organic is expensive so do not let this be a deterrent of living yeast free. With or without organic you will see so many health improvements living yeast free. We recommend eating organic when you can financially and practically. We recommend using organic meat in our recipes but do not specifically call for it in each recipe.

What you can eat during Phase I

Meats:

Free range chicken, beef liver, chicken liver, bacon, beef, buffalo, pork, duck, goat, goose, ham, pheasant, quail, spare ribs (no sauce), Veal, Venison, Hen, free range eggs. Choose organic meat whenever you can.

Bologna, frankfurters, sausage, and salami can be eaten occasionally. Read the labels avoid if contains: starches, sugar and fructose.

When buying deli meat, buy it fresh and check the sugar count should be less than 3 g per serving.

Grass fed beef is best because of its fat profile and also because a grass diet consists of fresh grass. The alternative diet for cattle consists of moldy grains, corn and other miscellaneous not-specified feed. Remember, you are what you eat and you are what you eat ate. Let's keep the mold out of our diets as much as possible.

Limit intake on red meats and pork.

Fish:

Anchovy, caviar, herring, mussel, sardine, abalone, arctic char, clam, crayfish, crab, lobster, octopus, oyster, mercury free wild salmon, scallop, shrimp, snail, squid, catfish, cod, flounder, grouper, haddock, mahi mahi, perch, red snapper, black cod, scrod, sole, tilapia, trout, turbot, and white sea bass.

No fish with high mercury levels such as tuna, shark, Atlantic salmon.

Vegetables:

All herbs, asparagus, green beans, bok choy, broccoli, green and red cabbage, sauerkraut, savoy cabbage, cauliflower, celery, chili pepper, green chili peppers, cucumber, eggplant, endive, escarole, fennel, kale, all lettuce, fresh maitake mushrooms, okra, onions, green onions, green peas, snow peas, green and red peppers, jalapeno peppers, radicchio, radishes, rhubarb, shallots, spinach, spaghetti squash, summer squash, swiss chard, tomato, turnips, and watercress.

Carrots you can eat raw, one to two times daily.

Only Maitake mushrooms because they are low carb. Fresh only, not dried.

Avoid potatoes, which are basically just sugar.

Nuts:

Eat unsalted almonds, hazel, flax seeds, macadamia, pecan, pine nuts, pumpkin seeds, sesame, sunflower seeds, chestnuts and walnuts.

Essential Fats:

Real butter, cream, ghee, plain Greek yogurt, kefir, avocado, coconut, olives, coconut oil (which kills yeast), flax seed oil, macadamia oil, olive oil, pumpkin seed oil, sesame oil and walnut oil.

Fruits:

You can only have one serving of fruit per day. If you notice any of these fruits are making you feel sick your body is telling you no.

Fresh apricots and fresh plums

1 cup serving size: blackberries, blueberries, cherries, cranberries, papaya, raspberries, strawberries, and green apples.

1 cup of tomato, unsweetened grapefruit (1-2 a week), lemon, and lime juice

Grains:

No Grains during this phase because they are high in carbs

Drinks:

Coconut Milk, heavy whipping cream, almond milk (all unsweetened)

Distilled water to keep the body flushed of toxins.

Club Soda (if you get flavored, make sure no artificial ingredients)

Vitamin Water (low carb) sweetened with Stevia.

Extra Tips:

If you have 3 meals a day limit snacks to 1-2 a day.

There is a must have drink called Kombucha: Gingerade. You can find it at Wholefoods or at your health food store. It is a probiotic and really helps with transitioning in to this diet. It is a great treat on its own and also makes excellent dressings, dips, etc. Get creative!

Natural peppermint tea will be very soothing on your digestive system while on the candida yeast diet. It helps kill yeast as well as soothing nausea, abdominal fullness, or pain. Try to drink four 8-ounce glasses of distilled water a day, and four glasses of bottled, reverse osmosis, or spring water to keep the body flushed of toxins.

Cravings and Symptoms:

Cravings are a part of detox. We promise you it will get easier and easier. By not cheating you will kill the yeast and minimize cravings.

If you feel nauseous; use ginger or peppermint mints or tea.

If you have headaches; use peppermint oil and rub on temples of your head.

If you are hungry grab a snack and you can eat as late as you want but DO NOT CHEAT. Grab some turkey, some veggies, nuts or leftovers but just don't cheat.

In the beginning you may have less energy because you are detoxing. This is normal, so take it easy on yourself. If you do decide to work out make sure you do not overdo it. We could not work in the beginning of this journey. The energy will come....just wait for it.

Phase II - The Recovery Phase

Phase II is the recovery phase. You are almost there! The point of this phase is to see what you can add back into your diet without feeling sick and bloated- the symptoms of bad yeast. Pay attention to your body. Listen to what it is telling you. Right now it is important to boost your immune system after killing the yeast. Be slow to add new things back into your diet. Continue to take your supplements that were suggested in Phase I.

Be careful when adding carbs and grains back into your diet. These grains should be added back very slowly. When starting phase II, try adding back one item from the following list 1 time per week for 1 month to see how your body handles carbs.

Carbs - slowly add back in to your diet:

Amaranth
Quinoa
Kamut
Millet
Basmatti rice
Wild rice (look for wild rice only, not mixed with other types of rice)
Black Beans
Fruits (Pears, Pineapple can be added, just hold off on the rest until Phase III)
Rolled Oats
Carrots
Yams (1 serving per week)
Freshly Squeezed Juices (start with one time a week)

It is still a good idea to restrict fruit but not as much as in Phase I. It is best to eat fruit in the morning. Phase II is just as important as Phase I, so you must follow through and slowly add the right foods back into your diet to feel the benefits of yeast free living. When you add back in an item from this list make sure the serving size is under 20 grams of carbs.

Lifestyle Phase

Welcome to your new lifestyle!! Congratulations! How do you feel? Advancing to this phase is different for everyone and you will be wondering how to know when to move into the lifetime phase? Trust the process and you will know. If you are unsure, you probably are not ready. That should encourage you. Your body will tell you when you are ready. If you don't feel better or your symptoms are not improving, stay in Phase II. It is not good to just start eating or drinking what "other" people eat after living yeast free.

Many people want to know about alcohol consumption while living yeast free. It should probably be avoided to maintain a healthy lifestyle but if you are going to sparsely drink, wait until your health symptoms improve and then slowly add back in the following, which have very few calories and/or low carbs.

Whiskey, Gin, Brandy, Rum and some Vodka less than an ounce

Less than 5 ounces of Red Wine

Other Foods you can add back in:

Amaranth Flour

Bananas

Baking Soda

Beans (canned)

Breads, gluten free and unyeasted

Coconut Flour

Almond Flour

Tapioca Flour

Teff Flour

Crackers, Rye (Yeast Free)

Dark Chocolate (unsweetened, organic over 75%),

Decaf Coffee

Legumes

Milk (organic Whole)

Milk Substitutes

Oranges

Popcorn (natural)

Salmon

Seaweeds

Coconut Aminos

Tuna

V-8 Juice

Vinegar (limited)

Goat Cheese (Raw is best)

This is all about learning! Yeast free living can be fun and delicious especially with the help of this cookbook.

Helpful Tips:

Grocery Store

It can be frustrating to get your grocery list together and then to find many of your ingredients unavailable at your store. Many of the items in phase I must be found at a health food store or specialty stores such as Wholefoods or Trader Joe's. I would recommend carving out enough time to go to a health food store and a regular store to save money and to stock up on hard to find ingredients. If you plan ahead you won't be so frustrated. There are also great websites to purchase these things at wholesale cost. If you cannot afford organic meat, start with what you can. You still will see a great improvement in your health.

Farmers Market

Going to the local farmers market can help save money when buying lots of fresh ingredients. Getting your fruits and vegetables, and sometimes oil, can cut your grocery bill in half. Also, depending on where you live, you can find local farmers that have organic meat that you can buy in bulk to save money.

Refrigerating, Freezing and Storing

Many of our recipes in this cookbook are freezer friendly. Soups and all other cooked food recipes will freeze well. You can double up batches and save time by just unthawing week to week instead of having to make the same batches each week.

Kitchen Essentials

There are a few items that will save you lots of time with many of these recipes. The first thing needed is a food processor. They are affordable and will help with many of these recipes. For whipping cream you can use a hand held beater or a mixer. To mince garlic you can use a glass cup and press down on the garlic. These tricks will save you time without breaking the bank. We are not big "gadget" people, so skip the fancy gadgets, and stick to a few essentials. A wooden spoon and a sharp knife will be your new BFFs.

For more suggestions and recipes please follow

livingyeastfree.com & **yeastfreekitchen.com**

For any health concerns please consult your primary physician.

.

Breakfast

Cherry Claflouti

3 cups frozen cherries, thawed
1/2 cup almond flour
3 eggs
1/4 cup Greek yogurt
1/4 cup coconut milk
1 tbsp butter
1 tsp vanilla extract or 1 drop essential oil

Preheat oven to 375 F. Butter a 10-inch pie pan and then arrange the thawed cherries in a single layer on the bottom of the pan. Beat the eggs in a bowl for one minute and whisk in the yogurt, coconut milk, and vanilla. Whisk in the flour and pour mixture over the cherries. Dot the top with the butter and bake until golden brown, about 40 minutes.

Oatmeal

1 cup unsweetened almond milk
1 cup water
1/2 tsp kosher salt
1 tsp vanilla extract or 1 drop essential oil
1 cup old-fashioned gluten free rolled oats
Your favorite fruit or toppings

Set a saucepan over high heat. Pour in the unsweetened almond milk and water. Add the salt and vanilla extract. Bring the liquids to a boil. Once liquid is boiling add the oats. Stir rapidly until water is boiling again and then turn the heat to low. Keep oats on low or simmer continuing to stir until the oats are creamy and liquid is absorbed. (This will take 15-20 minutes). Cover the pan; turn off heat and let set for a few more minutes to absorb rest of liquid. Top with your favorite toppings.

Quiche

1 cup broccoli (or other vegetable choice)
6 eggs
1 cup heavy cream or 1 1/2 cups coconut milk
1/2 tsp nutmeg
1/2 tsp salt
1/4 tsp pepper
1/4 cup goat cheese (optional)
Butter (to coat baking dish)

Preheat oven to 425 F. Cook the vegetables in a skillet, steamer or microwave first (beginner cooks can pick up a fresh steam bag and follow directions). Whisk eggs, cream, seasonings in a bowl. Add vegetables and goat cheese to the mixture and put in a 10 inch round buttered baking dish. Bake for 22-24 minutes until the middle is set.

Egg Muffins

8 eggs
1/3 pound cooked meat (bacon, sausage or turkey)
1 pepper (red or orange), finely chopped
1/4 tsp oregano
Salt and pepper to taste
Coconut oil (to grease muffin pan)

Grease muffin pan with coconut oil. Preheat oven to 350 F. Whisk the eggs in a bowl and add all remaining ingredients. Use 1/4 cup measuring cup to scoop into muffin pan. Bake for 20 minutes or until a toothpick can easily come in and out of muffin.

Spinach Frittata

1 1/4 cups ground meat (sausage, turkey, bacon or beef)
1 1/2 cups spinach
1 tomato diced
8 eggs, beaten
2 tsp oregano
1/2 cup feta cheese (optional)

Preheat oven broiler to high. In a skillet heat coconut oil over high heat, add meat and cook until lightly browned. Turn heat down to medium, add tomatoes. Cook tomatoes for a few minutes and then add beaten eggs and sprinkle with spinach and oregano. Stir fast, then let cook until the eggs set. Sprinkle the cheese on top and put in oven for 5 minutes. When Frittata is golden brown it is done.

Green Eggs and Ham

1/4 cup heavy cream
8 eggs
2 cups fresh spinach, chopped
1 lb. cooked sausage, chopped in small pieces
3 tbsp pesto (recipe in appetizer & dips)

Preheat oven to 350 F. Whisk eggs and heavy cream for about one minute. Add spinach, sausage and pesto then pour mixture into a well-greased 12-muffin tin. Bake for about 40 minutes.

Appetizers & Dips

Pesto

3 cups fresh basil leaves
1/2 cup fresh parsley
1/4 cup pine nuts
1/4 cup olive oil
4 cloves garlic
1 tsp cumin

Combine all ingredients in the food processor and blend until smooth. Use in a recipe, for a veggie dip or use for a salad dressing.

Guacamole

2 avocados, peeled, pitted and cut into chunks
1 lemon, juiced
2 cloves of garlic, minced
Salt and pepper to taste
1 tomato, diced

Mash avocados, lemon, garlic together in a bowl until smooth. Add salt, pepper and tomatoes.

Tzatziki

3 tbsp olive oil
2 cloves garlic, minced finely
1/4 tsp salt and pepper, each
2 cups Greek yogurt
2 cucumbers, peeled, seeded and diced
1 tsp chopped fresh dill

Slowly whisk together olive oil, garlic, salt, pepper and Greek yogurt in a bowl. Stir in cucumber and dill. Chill for one hour before serving.

Blueberry Balls

3-5 pitted dates
1 cup walnuts
1/2 cup pecans
1 tbsp coconut oil
1/2 cup fresh blueberries
3/4 cup unsweetened coconut

Put dates, walnuts, and pecans in a food processor. Pulse to a pasty consistency, add coconut oil and a 1/4 cup of shredded coconut. Transfer paste to a bowl, mix in blueberries. Spoon and roll into twelve balls. Roll the balls in the remaining 1/2 cup of coconut. Chill and serve.

Chocolate Banana Muffins

3/4 cup coconut flour
1/2 tsp baking soda
1/4 tsp salt
6 eggs
1/2 cup melted coconut oil
1/2 cup raw honey
1 tsp vanilla extract or 1 drop essential oil
2 over-ripe bananas, mashed
1 cup chopped pecans
4 oz dark chocolate, roughly chopped

In a small bowl, combine dry ingredients. In a medium bowl, whisk eggs for one minute, add melted coconut oil, honey and vanilla. Combine the egg mixture with the dry ingredients and mix well. Let batter sit for 5 minutes. Add bananas, pecans and chocolate to the mix. Pour mixture into well-greased muffin tin. Bake at 350 F for 18-22 minutes, or until fork comes out clean. Makes 12 muffins, store in fridge.

Zucchini Chips and Buffalo Ranch Dip

2 zucchinis
2 tbsp coconut oil
Sea salt
1-3 red chili peppers, depending on how spicy you want your dip
1 bunch scallions, chopped
3 cloves garlic, minced
2 tbsp fresh chopped dill
3/4 cup Greek yogurt
1/4 cup heavy cream

Preheat Baking Stone or Pizza Stone at 450 F. Slice both zucchinis in 1/4 inch slices using a mandolin slicer or sharp knife. Lightly coat zucchini slices with 1 tbsp of melted coconut oil, generously salt with sea salt, and place the slices on the preheated stone in the oven. Bake until brown and crispy, about 20 minutes. Cool on a wire rack and serve immediately. They are best when they are almost burnt.

Buffalo Ranch Dip: Sauté chili peppers, scallions and garlic in 1 tbsp coconut oil for 3 minutes on medium heat. Remove from heat and let cool to room temperature. Put the cooled pepper mixture into a food processor and blend until smooth but slightly chunky. Mix in yogurt, dill and heavy cream.   Chill and serve.

Crunchy Prosciutto Chips with Dill Dip

6 oz. super thin-sliced prosciutto
1 cup Greek yogurt
2 tbsp water
1 tbsp lemon juice
2 tbsp fresh-snipped dill

Preheat oven to 350 F. Line a cookie sheet with parchment paper, lay prosciutto single-layered on the sheet and bake till crisp, about 8-10 minutes. Cool on wire rack.

Dill Dip: Mix yogurt, lemon juice, water and dill. Serve cold.

Tapenade

4 cloves garlic
1/2 cup kalamata olives
1/2 cup olives
3 tbsp parsley
2 tbsp lime juice
2 tbsp olive oil
Pinch of nutmeg

Blend all ingredients in food processor until finely chopped. Don't let it go until it becomes paste! Serve with unyeasted rye crackers or endive, peppers or other veggies for dipping.

Ramaki

3 cans whole water chestnuts
1 lb. bacon, cut into 1/2 strips
1 jar coconut aminos (soy sauce substitute)
Toothpicks

Wrap each water chestnut in 1/2 strip bacon and secure with toothpick. Place in 9x13 baking dish. Pour entire bottle of coconut aminos over the top, cover with foil and refrigerate overnight. Remove ramaki from the aminos (discard remaining coconut aminos) and place them on a broiler pan. Bake at 400 F for 20 minutes. For extra crispy ramaki, broil for a few minutes more.

Jerk Jerky

1 lb. London broil steak - fat trimmed off
1/2 cup coconut aminos
2 tbsp jerk seasoning (recipe in spices)

Slice steak into very thin, even strips (about 1/4 - 1/8 inch thick). Mix coconut aminos and spice in a freezer bag. Add meet to freezer bag and massage for 2-3 minutes. Place in refrigerator and let marinate for 24 hours. Heat oven to 170 F. Remove meat strips from marinade and pat dry with paper towel. Place strips directly on oven racks, spaced evenly so not to touch. Prop oven door slightly open using a wooden spoon and bake for 8-10 hours, flipping meat strips about 1/2 way through.

Herbed Almonds

3 cups raw almonds
3 tbsp herbed garlic butter (recipe below)
Sea salt

In a large skillet, melt the herbed garlic butter over medium heat until the butter just starts to bubble. Toss in the almonds and sprinkle with sea salt. Cook for 8-10 minutes, or until almonds begin to darken and smell wonderful, stirring often with wooden spoon.

Herbed Garlic Butter

1 stick butter, softened
3 cloves garlic, minced
1-drop oregano essential oil (or 2 tbsp chopped fresh oregano)
2 drops rosemary essential oil (or 3 tbsp fresh chopped
        rosemary)

Mix it all together and serve with unyeasted rye crackers (or use it to sauté!).
Look for this in our recipes!

Lemongrass Garlic Butter

1 stick butter, softened
3 cloves garlic, minced
3 drops lemongrass essential oil
or
1/4 cup fresh chopped (or frozen, thawed) lemongrass

Mix it all together and serve with unyeasted bread or crackers (or use it to sauté!)
Look for this in our recipes!

Herbed Goat Cheese Truffles

(Serve with Unyeasted Rye Crackers on an Antipasti Tray)

4 oz. goat cheese, room temp
1 tsp. Italian seasoning
1/4 cup finely chopped pecans
Chia seeds, flax seeds or finely chopped pecans to rolling balls in

Mix goat cheese, seasoning and pecans. Chill in fridge for at least 30 minutes so that it will be easier to handle. Roll goat cheese mixture with hands to form 8-10 small balls, then roll each ball into seeds/nuts.

Layered Taco Dip

1/2 lb. ground turkey
2 tbsp chili/taco seasoning (recipe in spices)
1/2 cup Greek yogurt
1 avocado, mashed
1 cup fresh chopped spinach or lettuce, chopped
1 cup grape tomatoes, chopped
1/2 small red onion, chopped
1/2 bunch cilantro, chopped
1/2 cup black olives

Brown ground turkey with chili/taco seasoning, let cool. While cooling, mix mashed avocado and Greek yogurt with remaining chili/taco seasoning. Combine the two. Spread turkey yogurt mixture on a plate or platter, then sprinkle spinach, tomatoes, onion, cilantro and olives over top. Serve with yeast free chips, plantain chips or veggies for dipping.

Meatball Lollipops

1 lb. ground sirloin
1 small onion, small diced
3/4 cup baby spinach, small chopped
2 cloves garlic, minced
1 tbsp Italian seasoning (recipe in spices)
1 egg, beaten
15-20 lollipop sticks (you can find these in craft stores)

Preheat oven to 375 F. Put all ingredients in a bowl and mix well using your hands. Form into 2 inch balls and place on a foil lined cookie sheet. Bake for 25 minutes. After you take them out of the oven to cool, firmly place a lollipop stick into each, making sure to insert it at least half way through the meatball but not all the way through.

If you prefer to make smaller meatballs instead of Lollipops, simply preheat the oven to 400 F, form the meat into 1 inch balls instead of 2, and bake for 20 minutes.

Chimichurri

1 cup cilantro
1 cup parsley
6 cloves garlic
1 small red onion
4 tbsp lime juice
2 tsp Italian seasoning (recipe in spices)
1 tbsp olive oil
1/4 cup water

Pulse first 6 ingredients in a food processor till chopped. Add water, then turn food processor on and slowly add oil until blended. It should be lumpy.

Turkey Meatball Lollipops

1 lb. ground turkey

1 small onion, small diced

2 cloves garlic, small minced

1 drop thyme essential oil or 1 tsp thyme

1 drop rosemary essential oil or 1 tsp rosemary

1 egg, beaten

15-20 lollipop sticks (you can find these in craft stores)

Preheat oven to 375 F. Put all ingredients in a bowl and mix well using your hands. Form into 2 inch balls and place on a foil lined cookie sheet. Bake for 25 minutes. After you take them out of the oven to cool, firmly place a lollipop stick into each, making sure to insert it at least half way through the meatball but not all the way through.

If you prefer to make smaller meatballs instead of Lollipops, simply preheat the oven to 400 F, form the meat into 1-inch balls instead of 2, and bake for 20 minutes.

Cranberry Sauce

(Serve with Turkey Meatball Lollipops)

One bag fresh cranberries
Juice of one orange (about 1/3 cup)
2 tbsp Pineapple juice
1/2 cup finely chopped pineapple
6 oz. fresh raspberries
1/3 cup water
1/2 cup chopped pecans

Simmer cranberries in water and juice, stirring occasionally, until they all pop open. Mash in pineapple and raspberries with a wooden spoon and then add chopped pecans. Cool and refrigerate for 4 hours before serving. If it is too tart for your taste, add stevia, honey or xylitol.

8 asparagus spears
2 oz. goat cheese, room temp
1 clove garlic, minced
1 tsp lemon juice
1 tbsp fresh snipped thyme
8 slices prosciutto

Blanch asparagus by immersing the spears in boiling water for 45 seconds and then transfer to a bowl of ice water until the spears are cool. Remove the spears from ice water, pat dry with a paper towel and set aside. In a small bowl, combine goat cheese, garlic, lemon juice and thyme. Spread goat cheese mixture evenly on the prosciutto slices and then wrap each asparagus spear in the prepared prosciutto slices.

Soups and Salads

Tomato Basil Soup

3 tbsp butter
2 onions, chopped
3 cloves garlic, minced
1 tbsp smoked paprika
3 1/2 cups beef or chicken broth
1 28 oz. can organic tomatoes
1/2 cup heavy cream
1/2 cup fresh basil, chopped or 2-3 drops basil essential oil
Salt and pepper to taste

In a large pot, sauté the onions and garlic in the butter until translucent. Stir in tomatoes and bring to a simmer. Then add broth and seasoning, and again bring to a simmer. Remove from heat, add cream, and transfer in small batches to a food processor and blend until smooth (or use an immersion blender). Stir in fresh basil and serve.

Broccoli Goat Cheese Soup

1 head of cauliflower florets
1 head broccoli florets
3 tbsp butter
2 cloves garlic, minced
1 onion, diced
2 leeks, chopped
3 cups chicken broth
4 oz. goat cheese

First, steam the broccoli florets and set aside. Sauté onions and garlic with the butter in a large pot until translucent. Add broth and bring to a boil, then add leeks and cauliflower. Simmer until cauliflower is fork tender. Add in goat cheese and stir until it melts, and then let cool slightly. Blend with immersion blender or in a food processor until smooth and creamy. Remember those steamed broccoli florets? Toss them in and enjoy warm.

Moroccan Chili

1 lb. stew meat
1 lb. ground turkey
1/2 cup onion
2 tbsp Moroccan spice (recipe in spices)
1 can white beans, drained and rinsed
28 oz. diced tomatoes
8 oz. tomato paste

Brown ground turkey and stew meat with Moroccan spices and onion. Add diced tomatoes and tomato paste and beans, bring to a simmer. Serve hot.

Boyfriend Chili

1 lb. beef
1 can diced tomatoes
1 can tomato sauce
2 tbsp chili/taco seasoning (recipe in spices)
3 cloves garlic, minced
1 tbsp cumin

Brown the beef in a hot Skillet. Add all ingredients including brown beef in to stovetop or Crock Pot and let simmer for a few hours and serve.

Jambalaya

1 lb. sausage
2 tbsp olive oil
1 small sweet onion, diced
2 cups celery, diced
1 red pepper, diced
1 green pepper, diced
3 cloves garlic, minced
4 tsp Cajun seasoning (recipe in spices)
28 oz. diced tomatoes
1 cup chicken broth
1 1/2 lb. cooked shrimp

Cook the sausage in oil on med-high heat until browned, remove from pan and set aside. Add onion, celery, peppers, garlic and seasoning into the leftover oil in the pan. Sauté for 5 minutes. Stir in tomatoes and broth and simmer for 20 minutes. Add shrimp and sausage, cook for 5 minutes more.

Enchilada Soup

2-3 lbs chicken breast
1 green pepper, chopped
1 4-oz can chopped jalapenos
1 4-oz can chopped green chilies
2 tbsp coconut oil
1 14-oz can diced tomatoes
1 7-oz can tomato sauce
3 cloves garlic, minced
1/2 tbsp cumin
1 1/2 tbsp chili powder
2 tsp oregano
Salt and pepper to taste
Cilantro for garnish if desired
Dollop of Greek yogurt for topping if desired

Cook your chicken breasts separately, cut chicken into strips.
Put all ingredients in crock-pot. Cook on low for 8 hours or on
high for 6 hours. Serve and add cilantro topping and Greek yogurt
if desired.

Asparagus Soup

3 tbsp butter
2 cloves garlic, minced
1 onion, diced
2 tbsp Italian seasoning (recipe in spices)
2 1/2 cups chicken broth
2 lb. asparagus, chopped
1 can coconut milk

Melt butter in a big soup pot and sauté garlic and onion till translucent. Stir in seasoning, broth, asparagus, salt and pepper and bring to a boil. Turn heat down to medium and simmer until asparagus is tender, about 10 minutes. Add coconut milk and remove from heat. In small batches, blend in a food processor until smooth, or blend with immersion blender.

Saffron Squash Soup

2 lb. butternut squash
1 yellow onion
3 cloves garlic
2 tbsp butter
2 tsp saffron powder
1/2 tsp cinnamon
2 cups beef broth
1 can coconut milk

Preheat oven to 375 F. Cut squash in half-length wise, remove seeds and pulp, and place cut side down directly on oven rack and bake until fork tender, about 35 minutes. Sauté onion and garlic in the butter in a big soup pot until translucent. Add broth, saffron, salt and pepper and cinnamon, then bring it to boil. Add the cooked squash in chunks. Add the coconut milk and remove from heat. Blend well with immersion blender, food processor or blender.

If you would like, toast the seeds from the squash and garnish your soup with them. We like to bake them with olive oil, cinnamon and sea salt in the oven at 375 F for about 15 minutes.

Pumpkin Soup

6 cups chicken broth
2 tsp salt
4 1/2 cups pumpkin puree
1 tsp fresh parsley, chopped
1/2 tsp fresh thyme, chopped
1 clove garlic, minced
1/2 cup heavy cream
5 whole peppercorns

Heat the broth, salt, pumpkin, thyme, parsley, garlic and pepper-corns. Bring to a boil and then simmer for 30 minutes uncovered. Puree the soup using an immersion blender or food processor. After you have blended the soup, bring the soup to a boil again. Then reduce heat and simmer for another 30 minutes uncovered. Mix in the heavy cream. Pour into soup bowls and garnish with fresh parsley.

Leek Soup

2 leeks
1 onion (red or white)
3 cups chicken broth
3 stalks celery
1 tsp ginger powder
1 tsp chili powder
3 cloves garlic, minced
1/4 tsp salt
1/4 tsp pepper
1 chicken breast (optional)

Chop onion and celery in a food processor. Cut up leeks into fine pieces. Put chicken stock on stove over high heat and once boiling add leeks and onion and celery. Then add the rest of the ingredients. After 10 minutes put on simmer and put a lid on for 20 minutes. Then you may eat as is or use an immersion blender to smooth the soup. Enjoy.

Lemon, Basmati and Meatball Soup

1 lb. ground chicken
1 large egg, lightly beaten
1 tsp kosher salt
4 tsp loosely packed lemon zest, divided
1 tsp dried crushed rosemary, divided
3 tbsp olive oil, divided
1 medium sweet onion, chopped
3 carrots, thinly sliced
2 garlic cloves, minced
2 (32 oz.) containers chicken broth
5 -6 tbsp lemon juice
3/4 cups cooked basmati rice
1/2 cup fresh flat-leaf parsley leaves

Put all ingredients except chicken into Crock Pot and mix well.
Form ground chicken into 1 inch meatballs and drop into the
Crock Pot mixture and cook on low for 8 hours or high for 6 hours
and serve.

Egg Drop It Like It's Hot!! Soup

4 cups chicken broth

2 chicken breasts, cooked and cut into small pieces

2 cups of cauliflower (and/or broccoli)

4 eggs, beaten

2 tsp salt

1 tsp pepper

1 tsp oregano

Put all the ingredients in a crock pot and put in the refrigerator overnight. Next day put on low for 6 hours or high for 4 hours and serve.

Coconut Chicken Soup

2 lbs chicken, cooked
2 tbsp coconut oil
1 medium onion, diced
2 cloves garlic, minced
1 pepper, diced
2 jalapenos, diced
1/4 cup fresh cilantro, chopped
1-16 oz can diced tomatoes
1-15 oz can coconut milk
1 tbsp chili/taco season (recipe in spices)
1 lime, juiced
Salt and pepper to taste

Heat onions and peppers in the coconut oil for 3 minutes in a sauce pan over medium heat until onions are translucent. Then, add garlic, tomatoes, chicken, and cilantro and simmer for 5 minutes. Add in the coconut milk and jalapenos and simmer for another 5 minuets allowing flavors to cook together Add the rest of the ingredients, cook for two more minutes and enjoy. Serve immediately.

Pomegranate Pear Salad

4 large handfuls baby spinach
4 pears, thinly sliced
1 large pomegranate, seeds only
1/2 sweet onion, thinly sliced
3 tbsp olive oil
3 tbsp lemon or lime juice
1 drop thyme essential oil or 1 tbsp fresh snipped thyme

Whisk olive oil, lemon/lime juice and thyme together for dressing. Put spinach in a large bowl and toss with the dressing. Pile spinach on a platter. Arrange pears and onion on top of spinach and pour pomegranate seeds over the top and serve.

Mexican Salad

1 head lettuce, cut and washed
1 dollop Greek Yogurt
1/2 cup fresh salsa
1/2 cup homemade guacamole (recipe in appetizer & dips)
1 tomato, diced
1 lb. of beef, cooked

Arrange a bed of lettuce on a platter. Top with remaining ingredients and serve.

Minty Kale Salad

Salad:

3 cups chopped kale, rinsed and deveined
1/2 cup chopped fresh mint
1 cup blueberries
1/2 cup macadamia nuts, chopped

Dressing:

1/2cup Greek yogurt
Juice of 1 lime
Dash of white pepper

Mix all dressing ingredients in a bowl and toss with salad ingredients.

Chicken Salad Wraps

2 grilled chicken breasts, chopped into small pieces
1 1/2 cups homemade guacamole (recipe in appetizer & dips)
1 head romaine lettuce

Easy Peasy! Just mix the chopped chicken into the guacamole, wrap it up in a leaf of lettuce. Making this recipe is a great way to use leftover chicken and guacamole.

Caesar Salad

Salad:

1 head romaine lettuce, chopped
1/4 red onion, sliced thin
1 cucumber, sliced

Dressing:

1/2 cup Greek yogurt
1/4 tsp mustard powder
2 cloves garlic
1 tsp anchovy paste
2 tsp lime juice
2 tbsp olive oil
Salt and pepper

Blend garlic, mustard powder, anchovy paste, and lime juice in a food processor until smooth. Add in oil and blend until smooth. Fold in yogurt and mix the dressing with the romaine lettuce, onion and cucumber.

Citrus Salad With Avocado Cream Dressing

Salad:

4 large handfuls arugula mix
2 sliced oranges
2 sliced grapefruit
1/4-1/2 cup fresh-chunked coconut flesh

Pile Arugula Mix onto a platter. To chop oranges and grapefruit, cut top and bottom off each fruit, and then cut the peel off the sides. Slice into 1/4 inch rounds. Arrange them on top of arugula, drizzle dressing over top, and then sprinkle with fresh coconut.

Dressing:

1-2 ripe avocadoes
1/2 cup coconut cream/milk (use the cream top of the can first)
1/4 cup lime or key lime juice
1/2 bunch cilantro

Blend all ingredients in a food processor, adding more coconut milk if needed to get desired consistency.
Spice it up by tossing in a jalapeno if you like!

Mixed Pepper Salad

2 firm avocadoes, diced
1 1/2 cups cherry tomatoes, halved
1/2 red onion, diced
1/2 bunch cilantro
1/4 cup green peppers, diced
1/4 cup red pepper, diced
1/4 cup yellow pepper, dices
1/4 cup lime juice
1 tbsp chili/taco seasoning

Mix cherry tomatoes, onion, cilantro, peppers, lime juice and taco seasoning. Sprinkle avocadoes on top and serve.

Kale Salad

1 bunch kale
1-2 avocadoes, sliced and peeled
1/4 cup walnut oil
Juice from a whole lemon
Salt and pepper to taste
Walnuts (optional)

Blend together juice and oil in a bowl. Remove the rib from the kale (middle stem of kale) and thinly slice the kale leaves. Mix kale with avocado and dressing and season with salt and pepper. Top with walnuts for an extra crunch.

Side Dishes

Stuffing

1 lb turkey sausage, cooked, drained (crumble into small pieces)
2 leeks
1 yellow onion
2 stalks celery
2 tbsp olive oil
3 cups almond flour
5 eggs
1/2 cup chicken broth
1 tsp baking soda
2 tsp sea salt
1 tbsp sage
1 tbsp rosemary
1 tbsp thyme

Preheat oven to 350 F. On medium-high heat sauté the onion, celery and leeks in a skillet until tender. Then turn to high heat until well browned or slightly charred but not burnt. Set aside. In a large bowl, combine the almond flour, salt, baking soda, and spices. In a medium bowl, whisk together the eggs and broth, and then pour into the almond flour mixture. Mix until moistened. Stir in the sautéed mix and the cooked turkey sausage and pour into a buttered 9x13 pan and bake for 45-55 minutes, or until inserted toothpick comes out clean and top is very well browned. Cool slightly on a wire rack. Once it is cool enough to handle, break the "cake" into small stuffing-sized pieces with your hands or scramble the whole thing with a fork. Enjoy!

Ginger Slaw

1 bag shredded cabbage/slaw mix
1/2 cup unsweetened toasted coconut flakes or fresh coconut
3/4 cup coconut cream from top of can
3/4 cup kombucha gingerade
1 tbsp fresh grated ginger root
Sesame seeds for sprinkling

In large bowl, mix cabbage and coconut flakes. In small bowl combine coconut cream, Kombucha and fresh ginger, whisk together. Pour Kombucha mixture over the slaw and serve with sesame seeds sprinkled over top.

Chopped Olive Salad

(Serve on top of Burger)

1 cup roughly chopped kalamata olives
1 cup roughly chopped green olives
2 cloves garlic, minced
1/2 cup capers
Fresh pepper
Pinch of cumin
1 tbsp lemon juice

Just mix it all together and serve on top of a juicy burger.

Baked or Roasted Kale

Fresh head of kale
Olive oil
Salt

Preheat oven to 375 F. Cut up kale and take out the rib. (the rib is the center stem of the kale). Cut kale in to medium size pieces and wash. Towel dry the kale. Put kale in to a bowl and mix with 1 tablespoon of olive oil and blend well with hands. Then put kale onto a baking sheet so all kale is lying evenly on baking sheet in a single layer. Sprinkle salt on the kale. Cook for 8 minutes and flip kale over. Bake another 8-10 minutes until crispy but not burnt. Watch carefully.

Roasted Squash

1 Butternut squash – peeled, seeded and cut into 1 inch-cubes
2 tbsp olive oil
2 cloves garlic, minced
Salt and ground black pepper to taste

Preheat oven to 400 F. Toss butternut squash with olive oil and garlic in a large bowl. Season it with salt and pepper. Arrange coated squash on a baking sheet. Roast in the preheated oven until squash is tender and lightly browned, 25-30 minutes.

Cajun Spiced Spaghetti Squash

1 spaghetti squash
4 tbsp coconut oil
2-3 tbsp Cajun seasoning (recipe in spices)
2 cups broth (chicken, beef or vegetable)

Preheat oven to 450 F. Cut your spaghetti squash in half length-wise and discard seeds. Dot the coconut oil in both halves equally and sprinkle with the Cajun seasoning. Place both halves in a deep baking dish and pour the broth into them. Cover with foil and bake for 45-55 minutes, or until fork tender. While still in the shell, scrape into strands using a fork. Sprinkle with additional Cajun seasoning, if desired.

Lemongrass Green Beans

4 big handfuls fresh, crisp green beans
1-2 tbsp lemongrass garlic butter (recipe in appetizers and dips)
Water
Sea salt

In saucepan with lid, boil water. Toss in green beans and boil for 2 minutes. Remove from heat and drain, leaving green beans in the pan. Add lemongrass garlic butter. Put the lid on the pan to keep in the steam. Let rest until room temp and sprinkle with salt.

Mashed Cauliflower

1 medium head cauliflower
1 tbsp cream cheese, softened
1/2 tsp minced garlic
1/2 tsp of salt
1/8 tsp of pepper
1/2 tsp fresh or dry chives
3 tbsp unsalted butter

Set a large pot of water to boil over high heat. Clean and cut cauliflower into small pieces. Cook it in boiling water for about 6 minutes, or until well done. Drain well; do not let cool and pat cooked cauliflower very dry between several layers of paper towels. Puree the hot cauliflower with the cream cheese, garlic, salt and pepper until almost smooth. Garnish with chives, and serve hot with butter.

Steamed Asparagus

1 bunch of asparagus
1 tbsp olive oil
Salt and Pepper

Cut Asparagus stem off (about 1/4 inch off bottom). Cut asparagus in half and put in a frying pan on medium. Add olive oil and
salt and pepper and cook for about 5-8 minutes depending on
how crisp you want asparagus.

Perfect Asparagus

One bunch of fresh asparagus
2 tsp coconut oil
Water
Salt

In saucepan with lid, boil water. Toss in asparagus and boil for 1
1/2 to 2 minutes. Drain, then add coconut oil and stir. Put the lid
on the pan to keep in the steam. Let rest until nearly room temp
and sprinkle with salt.

Spinach You WANT To Eat

We eat this for breakfast often, since we already have a hot pan after frying an egg. Perfect.

A few big handfuls of baby spinach
1 tsp herbed garlic butter (recipe in appetizers and dips)
Pepitas (pumpkin seeds)

Heat herbed garlic butter over medium heat. Remove pan from heat. Throw a few handfuls of fresh baby spinach into the hot pan and toss with tongs until slightly wilted. Sprinkle with pepitas.

Cucumber Raita

(Yummy with Moroccan Tagine)

4 hothouse (seedless) cucumbers, peeled and shredded
2 cups Greek yogurt
3 tbsp lime juice
4 tbsp fresh mint, chopped (no substituting with dried mint!)
Dash of salt

Mix it all up in a bowl. Eat alone or serve with Moroccan Tagine. You can use it as a salad dressing, too. You may want to add heave cream for a dressing-like consistency.

Fennel Salad:

1 bulb fennel, thinly sliced
1 small white onion, thinly sliced
2 tbsp lemon juice
1 tbsp olive oil
3 tbsp fresh snipped dill
Fresh ground pepper

In a large bowl, combine fennel, onion and dill. In a separate bowl, whisk together lemon juice, olive oil and pepper in a bowl and pour over fennel mix.

Garlic Cheesy Biscuits

2 1/2 cups almond flour
1/4 tsp salt
1 tsp baking soda
3 tbsp butter
1/4 cup Greek yogurt
2 eggs
2 cloves garlic, minced
4 oz goat cheese

Preheat oven to 350 F. Make garlic butter by sautéing garlic in the butter until lightly browned, then set aside. Combine flour, salt and baking soda in a large bowl. In another bowl, combine the garlic butter that you just made, yogurt, and eggs and whisk to combine. Crumble in goat cheese, then combine with the dry mixture. Drop batter in scant 1/4 cups scoops, 2 inches apart, onto parchment lined baking sheet and bake for 15-20 minutes or until inserted toothpick comes out clean.

Ketchup

1 tbsp olive oil
1 small onion, diced
1 1/2 lb. roma tomatoes, chopped and peeled (or canned)
12 oz. tomato paste
1/4 tsp cayenne pepper
1/2 tsp cumin
1/2 tsp coriander
2 tsp garlic powder
3 tbsp honey (optional)

In a large pot, heat olive oil and sauté onion until translucent. Add all other ingredients and simmer on low-medium heat for 30 minutes. Cool slightly and blend with immersion blender or food processor. This makes LOTS of ketchup and freezes well in jars.

Mayo

1 egg yolk
1 cup olive oil
4 tsp lemon juice
Pinch of salt
Pinch of paprika

Whisk together egg yolk, lemon juice, salt and paprika until well combined. Continue whisking while slowly streaming in olive oil and continue to whisk until well blended. Alternatively use a food processor.

Turkey Gravy

Reserved pan juices from pan after roasting a turkey
2 tbsp almond flour OR coconut flour (We prefer almond flour)
1/2 cup water
Salt and pepper to taste

Pour in juices from turkey into a saucepan on medium heat. Gradually sprinkle in almond or coconut flour as needed to get the amount of thickness you are looking for. Gradually whisk in water until it thickens. Whisk on medium heat until gravy is warm and lump free.

Cocktail Sauce

3/4 cup ketchup (recipe in side dishes)
1/4 cup horseradish
2 tsp lime juice

Mix well and serve chilled. Spice it up with chili/taco seasoning if you're feeling saucy!

BBQ Sauce

1 tbsp coconut oil
2 cloves garlic, minced
1 cup coconut aminos
1 cup homemade ketchup (recipe in side dishes)
2 tbsp honey
1 tsp onion powder
1 tsp celery seed
1 tsp smoked paprika
1 tsp cumin

Sauté minced garlic in the coconut oil in a sauce pan over medium heat until slightly browned. Add all other ingredients and bring to a boil. Then reduce heat to low and simmer until thickened, about 30 minutes.

Main Courses

Chai Spiced Pork Tenderloin

2 lb. pork tenderloin, fat removed
1/4 cup olive oil
1/2 cup kombucha or strong brewed chai tea
5 chai tea bags
2 cups water

Put the olive oil and Kombucha or strong brewed chai tea into a large freezer bag. Remove the loose tea from 4 tea bags and rub contents onto the pork tenderloin and then place it in the bag with the olive oil. Let it marinade together in the fridge for 2-24 hours. Brew strong chai tea with the water and one tea bag and pour it into the crock-pot. Add the marinade and pork to the tea in the crock-pot and cook on low for 6-8 hours. We like to serve this with pears on the side (raw or roasted).

Cajun Red Snapper

4-6 oz. red snapper fillets
4 tbsp Cajun seasoning (recipe in spices)
8 tbsp melted coconut oil

Rub each fillet with 4 tbsp melted coconut oil and generously sprinkle them with Cajun spice on both sides. Heat the remaining 4 tbsp oil in a large heavy skillet over med-high heat. Once oil is hot, place fillets in skillet and cook the first side until blackened, about 5 minutes. Flip and cook an 2-3 minutes more or until fillets easily flake with a fork.

Creamy Shrimp and Veggies

2 tbsp olive oil
2 medium zucchini, sliced
3 cups broccoli florets, roughly chopped
2 cups cherry tomatoes
4 cloves garlic, minced
3/4 cup chicken broth
2 lb. large shrimp, cooked
4 oz. goat cheese
1 tbsp Cajun seasoning (recipe in spices)

Heat olive oil in large skillet over med-high heat. Add zucchini, broccoli and garlic then stir for 3-4 minutes. Add tomatoes and cook until they split, about 2-3 minutes. Add broth and bring to a simmer. Add goat cheese and Cajun seasoning and stir constantly until creamy. Add shrimp and cook for 2 more minutes. Serve warm.

Coconut Shrimp

Don't you just love the fried coconut shrimp that you get in restaurants? Us, too! Try this baked coconut shrimp recipe. You won't even miss the gluten and lard! We Promise!

1 lb. raw shrimp, cleaned, deveined and patted dry
2 cups coconut flakes, unsweetened (not the low fat kind)
3 tbsp melted coconut oil

Toast coconut in oven at 300 F, stirring every minute or so, until brown and toasted, about 5-8 minutes total. Set aside on a plate. Toss shrimp in a bowl with melted coconut oil to coat, and then roll shrimp in toasted coconut and place on cookie sheet lined with parchment paper. Bake at 400 F for 6-7 minutes; remove from oven and let sit till room temp.
Try this with Citrus Salad and Avocado Cream Dressing.

Blackened Chili Chicken

4 boneless, skinless chicken breasts
Olive oil
6-8 tbsp chili/taco seasoning (recipe in spices)

Preheat your grill to medium-high. Rub each chicken breast with olive oil and then rub with chili/taco seasoning. Grill chicken until internal temperature is 165 F and nicely browned on both sides.

Marinara!...and Spaghetti Squash

Really, this recipe is all about the Marinara. It is delicious over spaghetti squash, which is a family favorite because it's so much like traditional spaghetti, but you can serve it so many ways. Try it over meatballs with artichoke and olives. Yum! This recipe easily makes three batches, so I keep one batch fresh to use right away. Then I divide what is left into two gallon-size zipper bags and freeze them individually. To defrost, just lay the baggie on the kitchen counter for an hour or two.

1 spaghetti squash
3 tbsp butter
1 small sweet onion
4 cloves garlic
3 tbsp Italian seasoning (recipe in spices)
2 bay leaves
2 whole, trimmed celery stalks
28 oz. can whole tomatoes
28 oz. can tomato puree
Salt and pepper to taste

Cut spaghetti squash lengthwise and bake with the inside facing down directly on oven rack at 375 F for 35-45 minutes. Sauté onion, garlic and seasoning in butter until onion is translucent. Add both, cans of tomatoes, bay leaves, salt and pepper and whole celery stalks. Simmer on low heat stirring occasionally, for one hour. Remove bay leaves and celery stalks and discard them. Blend well with immersion blender or food processor.

Tilapia with Papaya Chutney

For tilapia:
3-4 tilapia fillets
1/2 lemon
3-4 tsp coconut oil
Salt and pepper

Preheat oven to 375 F. Dot each tilapia fillet with a tsp. of coconut oil, squeeze lemon over it and then sprinkle with salt and pepper. Bake for 20-25 minutes or until it flakes easily with a fork.

For Chutney:
2 cups papaya, chopped
2 plums, chopped
1 tbsp olive oil
1/2 onion
2 cloves garlic, minced
1/2 cup water
2 tsp grated ginger
1 bay leaf

Sauté onion, garlic and ginger in olive oil on medium heat for 2-3 minutes. Add water and bring to boil. Add all other ingredients and simmer until fruit is tender. Remove bay leaf and cool to room temp and serve.

Chicken Satay with Almond Sauce for Dipping

This is a yeast free friendly and much healthier version of the Asian classic. The Almond sauce lasts for weeks in the fridge.

3-4 boneless, skinless chicken breasts, cut into strips (skewers)

For chicken marinade combine these ingredients in food processor and blend well:

3 drops lemongrass essential oil or 1/4 cup fresh or frozen
    lemongrass, chopped
2 shallots or 1 small onion
3 cloves garlic
1 tsp cayenne pepper
1 tsp cumin
2 tbsp fresh ginger
2 tbsp coconut aminos
2 tbsp lime juice
1/4 cup water
Marinade the chicken for 2-24 hours, and then grill on skewers

For Almond Sauce:
1 cup natural almond butter
2/3 cup coconut milk
2 tsp coconut oil
Pinch of salt
2 tbsp coconut aminos
3 cloves garlic
2 tsp lemon juice
2 tsp fresh ginger

Blend all ingredients in food processor until well blended and consistency for dipping. If needed, add a little water.

Baked Whole Chicken

Whole chicken
6 tbsp butter, softened
3 tbsp snipped dill
1 tbsp lemon juice
1 tbsp lime juice
1 lemon
1 lime

Preheat oven to 450 F. Mix butter, dill, lemon juice and lime juice in a bowl. Loosen and lift the chicken's skin and rub butter mixture all over its body under the skin, keeping skin on the bird for cooking. Poke several holes with a fork in the lemon and the lime and stuff them into the chicken's cavity. Bake uncovered in a shallow baking dish for about one hour or until internal temp is 165.

Herbed Scallops

1/4 cup herbed garlic butter or lemongrass garlic butter or just plain butter if you must (recipes in appetizers and dips)
1 lb. scallops

Heat butter in a large skillet on med-high heat. Add the Scallops, flat side down. Do not move the scallops once they are placed! You want them to sit still on the pan to get that yummy butter crust. Let cook, undisturbed, for 3 minutes. Then flip each scallop over and cook for 2 minutes more.

Bacon Wrapped Chicken Thighs

4 chicken thighs, boneless and skinless
8 slices bacon
3 tbsp Moroccan spice (recipe in spices)

Preheat oven to 375 F. Rub spice into bacon strips, and then wrap them around the chicken thighs (2 strips per thigh). Secure with toothpicks if necessary. Bake for 35-45 minutes or until internal chicken temp is 165 F.

Flank Steak

Flank steak 1-2 lbs.
1 tbsp chili powder
1 tbsp espresso rub (found at store by the spices or grind your
    own beans)
Olive oil

Cut flank steak in strips. Blend chili powder and espresso rub to-gether. Rub on steak strips. Put rubbed steak in a sauté pan with olive oil on medium heat for 5-10 minutes until desired cooking temperature and enjoy.

Moroccan Lamb Tangerine

2 lbs. lamb, cubed
3 leeks
1 large sweet onion
2 cups chopped celery
16 oz. chicken broth
3 drops lemongrass essential oil
or
1/4 cup chopped fresh or frozen lemongrass
2-3 tbsp Moroccan spice (recipe in spices)

Put all ingredients in Crock Pot and stir. Cook on low for 6 hours.

Savory Chicken

1 4-5lb whole chicken (giblets removed)
2 lemons
Fresh bunch of basil
1 tbsp melted butter

Preheat oven to 350 F. Rinse chicken and pat dry. Put chicken in a baking pan. Cut two lemons in half and squeeze on chicken and in chicken. Place all fresh basil inside chicken and stuff squeezed lemons inside chicken. Take melted butter and rub all over outside of chicken. Cook for 1 1/2 to 2 hours at 350 F or until done.

Stuffed Chicken Pepper

4 large green, red or orange peppers
2 tbsp olive oil
1 medium onion, finely chopped
2 tsp minced garlic
2 cups diced cooked chicken
2/3 cup tomato sauce
1/4 tsp ground black pepper
1 cup cooked basmati rice

Preheat the oven to 375 F. Cut the tops off the peppers and re-move all seeds and middle (throw insides away). Put peppers in a cooking dish.

In a skillet heat olive oil to medium heat, sauté the onion and garlic and cook until tender. Put the onion and garlic in a bowl and stir in cooked chicken, tomato sauce, rice and black pepper. Scoop the mixture in the peppers and bake in oven for 35 minutes until the peppers are tender.

Zucchini Boats

1 lb. ground turkey or beef
1/4 cup pine nuts
1 clove garlic, minced
1 lemon, juiced
1/4 tsp salt
1/4 tsp pepper
6 zucchini
2 cups chicken or vegetable broth
1 tbsp olive oil
1 cup Greek yogurt
1 tomato, diced
1 small cucumber, diced
1 bunch cilantro

Preheat oven to 400 F. Brown Beef or Turkey in a sauce pan over medium heat. Add the Pine nuts, garlic, lemon juice , olive oil, salt and pepper and cook for about 5 minutes. Leave on low heat until ready to use. Leaving the stem on, cut a strip off the entire length of the zucchini, about a quarter inch deep. Then scoop out the insides leaving it hollow, like a boat. Arrange zucchini in a medium baking dish and pour the broth in the bottom of the dish. Stuff the zucchini with the meat mixture. Put in oven and bake 30 minutes or until the zucchini is tender. Take out of oven, put cilantro, Greek yogurt, tomatoes and cucumbers on top and serve.

Fish Boats

2 fillets mild white fish (found in the fresh fish section of grocery
    store and ask for mildest white fish)
4 cloves of garlic, minced
1 tsp oregano
1 lemon, juiced
1 tbsp olive oil

Preheat oven to 400 F. Place 1 piece of fish on a large sheet of
aluminum foil and make a foil boat (or bowl) for each fish. In a
mixing bowl, put minced garlic, extra virgin olive oil, oregano, and
juice from lemon. Blend together with a fork and pour equally in
fish boats. Close up foil , put on a baking sheet and place in ov-
en. Cook for 15-20 minutes or until fish is done and easily flakes
with a fork.

Chicken A La Easy

2 chicken breasts
Olive oil
1 cup Greek yogurt
1 cup fresh salsa

Cook chicken with olive oil in a sauté pan over medium heat.
Once chicken is cooked all the way through add Greek yogurt and
salsa. Cook for 5 more minutes and serve.

Cauliflower Tortillas

1 medium head of cauliflower
3 eggs
1/2 tsp salt

Preheat oven to 375 F. Rinse, cut and dry the cauliflower. Take off most of the stems of the cauliflower. Put cauliflower in a food processor and pulse until finely processed (looks like rice). Take the cauliflower and put in bowl and microwave for 3 minutes. Take out and stir and repeat. Once cauliflower is hot and cooked, take a dish cloth and squeeze to drain the cauliflower of any access water. You must squeeze out ALL water to get a good tortilla. Put cauliflower in a bowl and add eggs and salt. Mix really well until it looks like a batter. Spoon the batter onto parchment paper. Evenly spread the batter into 6 circles (you can also use a tortilla maker if you have one). It should make 6 tortillas. Bake for 16 minutes and flip over and cook for 3 more minutes. Remove from parchment and put on a cooling rack. You may make in bulk and freeze to pull out for tacos or sandwich wraps.

How does my pork butt look in this pan?

Boneless pork butt (3lb-9lb)
1 tbsp oregano
1 tsp pepper
1 lemon
Water

Preheat oven to 300 F. Cut raw boneless pork in to cubes. Place pork in a baking dish. Add oregano and pepper. Cut lemon in half and squeeze over pork. Throw lemon on top of pork. Add water 1/2 to 2/3 of the way to the top of the meat until meat is almost covered. Cover the dish with foil. Cook for 2 hours. Take foil off and leave in for one more hour. If you stab it with a fork and it falls apart, it is ready.

This is great for making in bulk and freezing. When reheating after freezing, just thaw and add a little olive oil to a saucepan to warm. Use as a main dish, with tacos or whatever you desire.

Pork Loin and Veggies Teriyaki

We love options! Here are two Teriyaki recipes for you to try; Raspberry for Phase One and Pineapple for Lifestyle Phase. Each of these recipes is easily enough for two family dinners, so when we make a batch we use ½ for dinner and then freeze the other half in a jar to use another time. To thaw, simply immerse the frozen jar in luke warm water for an hour or so.

For Pineapple Teriyaki:

1 cup coconut aminos

1 cup pineapple juice with pulp

1/2 tsp nutmeg

2 cloves garlic, minced

1 tbsp coconut oil

Sauté garlic in olive oil till browned. Add coconut aminos, nutmeg and pineapple juice, cook on low medium till thick and bubbly.

For Raspberry Teriyaki:

1 cup water

1 cup coconut aminos

12 oz. fresh raspberries (you could use blueberries instead)

2 cloves garlic, minced

2 tbsp fresh ginger, minced

1 tbsp coconut oil

Sauté ginger and garlic in coconut oil till browned, add raspberries and mash with wooden spoon. Add water and coconut aminos, cook low medium till thick and bubbly.

For the Pork Loin and veggies:

1 lb. thinly sliced pork loin (your butcher can slice it for you)
2 tbsp coconut oil
2 cups sugar peas, roughly chopped into large chunks
1 cup celery, chopped
1/2 red onion, thinly sliced
2 cans sliced water chestnuts

Heat coconut oil over med-high heat. Toss in the pork loin and cook for about 5 minutes, until browned. Add in sugar peas, celery, onion and water chestnuts and cook for about 2 minutes or until veggies are a little tender but still crisp. Pour in some teriyaki sauce to taste (about half a batch is best).

Crepes

1/2 cup coconut milk
2 tbsp butter, melted
4 tbsp coconut flour
8 egg whites

Sweet Filling:
1 tbsp butter
1 cup fresh berries
(Sauté the berries in the butter before placing on crepe)

OR

Savory Filling:
1/2 chicken breast, cooked, per crepe
Goat cheese (optional)
A handful of fresh spinach per crepe

In a large bowl, combine the coconut milk, butter and coconut flour with a whisk until it is smooth. Whisk egg whites separately until frothy and then combine into the coconut milk mix very slowly. Butter a skillet over medium heat. Cover the pan with batter just enough to thinly cover entire skillet. Swirl the batter around until it is all spread out. You can use a spatula to lift the batter after 1 minute to make sure it won't stick to skillet. After a couple minutes, when crepe is browned, flip it with a spatula. Cook for 2 more minutes, spread topping on half an then fold the crepe and slide it out of pan. ENJOY your delicious crepe for dessert, breakfast or dinner.

Crab Cakes

1 lb. cooked crab
1 small red onion, chopped
1 red pepper, chopped
1 yellow pepper, chopped
3 cloves garlic, minced
Coconut oil
4 tbsp Cajun spice, divided (recipe in spices)
2 tbsp lime juice
3 tbsp chopped parsley
1 tbsp water
1 1/2 cups crumbled unyeasted, gluten free crackers, divided
1 beaten egg
1/2 cup Greek Yogurt or mayo (recipe in dips)
Greek yogurt and additional Cajun spice for dip if desired

Preheat oven to 400 F. Sauté onion, peppers and garlic in coconut oil for 2-3 minutes, let cool. Mix crab, 2 tbsp of the Cajun spice, lime juice, parsley, and 3/4 cup of the crumbs in a separate bowl. Fold in sauté mixture. In a shallow dish, beat egg with water. In another shallow dish mix remaining crumbs with remaining Cajun seasoning. With your hands, form 1/3 cup patties with the crab mixture, lightly coat with egg mixture, and then coat patties in the crumb mixture. Place patties on a parchment lined baking sheet and bake for 15 minutes, or until browned. These freeze really well and thaw quickly at room temp.
Dip for Crab Cakes: Mix 1/2 cup Greek yogurt with Cajun spice to taste.

Spices

Italian Seasoning

1/4 cup onion powder
1/2 cup dried parsley
3 tbsp oregano
2 tbsp garlic powder
1 tbsp thyme
2 tsp celery seed
3 tsp minced onion

Moroccan Spice

1/4 cup nutmeg
1/4 cup cumin
1/4 cup coriander
2 tbsp Ginger
2 tbsp cinnamon
2 tbsp cardamom
1 tbsp cayenne pepper

Jerk Seasoning

3 tbsp thyme
3 tbsp garlic powder
3 tbsp onion powder
3 tbsp pepper
3 tbsp parsley
3 tbsp cumin
3 tbsp chives
2 tbsp ginger

Cajun Seasoning

1/4 cup paprika
2 tbsp onion powder
2 tbsp garlic powder
2 tbsp oregano
2 tbsp thyme
2 tbsp lemon peel (dehydrated)
2 tbsp crushed red pepper
2 tbsp minced onion

Mix well and store in an airtight container

Chili/Taco Seasoning

1/4 cup crushed red pepper
1/4 cup chili powder
2 tbsp garlic powder
2 tbsp onion powder
2 tbsp cumin
2 tbsp smoked paprika
2 tbsp oregano
2 tsp cayenne pepper

Mix well and store in an airtight container

Desserts

Key Lime Bars

For the Crust:

1/2 cup raw pecans

1/2 cup macadamia nuts

1/2 cup unsweetened coconut flakes

5 large dates

1 tbsp coconut oil

Pinch of salt

For the Filling:

1 1/2 cup raw cashew

2 tbsp coconut oil

2 tbsp honey

1 tsp vanilla extract or 1 drop essential oil

1/4 cup Greek yogurt

1/4 cup coconut cream from top of can

1/2 cup key lime juice

Line an 8x8-baking dish with parchment paper, set aside. Pulse all crust ingredients in a food processor, and then blend until it begins to stick together like dough. Press it into the bottom of prepared baking dish. Boil raw cashews for 20-25 minutes and then let cool. Next, put all filling ingredients into a food processor and blend until smooth and creamy. Spread over crust and freeze for 20-30 minutes. Serve.

Store in the freezer. Partially thaw for about 20 minutes before serving again.

Pumpkin Granola

2 cups oats
1 cup pecan pieces
2/3 cup unsweetened coconut flakes
2/3 cup pepitas (pumpkin seeds)
1/4 cup uncooked quinoa
1 tsp salt
4 tsp cinnamon
2 tsp ginger
2 tsp cardamom
2 tsp nutmeg
1/4 cup honey
2 egg whites
1/2 cup pumpkin puree
2 tsp vanilla extract or 2 drop essential oil
1/3 cup freshly squeezed orange juice or strong brewed tea
2 drops clove oil
1/4 cup melted coconut oil

Preheat oven to 325 F. Mix first 9 ingredients together in large bowl. In smaller bowl, whisk egg whites for one minute, then whisk in remaining ingredients. Combine both mixtures and stir to coat. Bake on a cookie sheet for 30-40 minutes, stirring every 10 minutes. It will crisp up after you take it out of the oven.

Pineapple Brule

4 pineapple rings, about 1 inch thick
1/4 to 1/2 cup heavy cream
1/4 cup stevia granules

Preheat oven on broil. Whip heavy cream until peaks form. Place pineapple rings on foil-lined baking sheet. Spread whipped cream on each and sprinkle with the stevia granules. Place the cookie sheet in oven about 4 inches from broiler, watching every second until brown and bubbly. Serve hot.

Baked Apples

4-5 apples, cored
2/3 cup pumpkin granola (recipe in desserts)
2 tbsp butter
1 cup strong brewed chai tea

Place cored apples in crockpot and fill each cored apple with pumpkin granola and top with the butter. Pour in chai tea. Cook on low for 4 hours. Leftovers make a super yummy breakfast.

Frozen Banana Bites

2 bananas
1 tbsp cashew or almond butter
3 tbsp heavy cream
3 tbsp butter
6 oz. dark chocolate

Slice bananas in 1/4 inch slices, then make a "sandwich" with cashew or almond butter between 2 banana slices, set aside. Simmer cream over low heat (careful not to burn), then add butter to melt, then add chocolate to melt, stirring constantly. Remove from heat, let it cool slightly, and then roll banana sandwiches to coat. Freeze on a cookie sheet lined with parchment paper. Enjoy frozen.

Lemon Mousse Parfaits

2 cups Greek yogurt
1/2 cup lemon juice
1/4-1/2 cup stevia
2 cups fresh blueberries or raspberries

Mix yogurt, lemon juice and stevia in a bowl. In 4 parfait glasses, layer lemon mixture and berries, alternating the two. Chill and serve.

Raspberry Coconut Macaroons

These macaroons are amazingly simple and delicious on their own. But, if you want to go crazy and drizzle them with a little melted chocolate for added flair, you have our blessing.

1 cup raspberries, room temperature
2 1/2 cups unsweetened coconut
2 egg whites
1 tsp vanilla extract or 1 drop essential oil
2 tsp stevia
Pinch of salt

Preheat oven to 325 F. Line cookie sheet with Parchment paper. Mix all ingredients together. With wet hands, form mixture into 1 inch balls and place on prepared cookie sheet. Bake for 16 minutes, rotating pan halfway through.

Chocolate Cake

1 lb. dark chocolate
1/4 cup butter
1/4 cup coconut oil
9 eggs (divided)
1/2 cup honey
1 tsp vanilla extract or 1 drop essential oil

Preheat oven to 350 F. Generously butter 9" spring form pan and set aside. Put chocolate, butter and coconut oil in a microwave safe bowl and microwave on LOW setting, stirring every 30 seconds, until melted. It doesn't take much heat to melt chocolate, so be careful not to burn it. In a separate bowl whisk egg yolks and honey together until well mixed, then mix in a small amount of the melted chocolate to "temper" the eggs (this will keep the heat of the hot chocolate from scrambling the eggs) and then whisk in the remaining chocolate. In another large bowl, beat egg whites until stiff peaks form and then fold in the chocolate mixture. Pour into prepared pan and bake 30-40 minutes, until cake top begins to crack and inserted toothpick comes out clean. Remove sides of pan after 10 minutes. Serve alone, with whipped cream, or hot fudge (see recipes).

Hot Fudge

5 oz. dark chocolate
4 tsp coconut oil
1/4 cup heavy cream
1/4 cup water

Melt chocolate and coconut oil in a microwave safe bowl on LOW setting, stirring every 30 seconds, until melted. Whisk in heavy whipping cream and water. Ta da!

Real Whipped Cream Topping

1 pint heavy whipping cream
1 tsp vanilla extract or 1 drop essential oil

Whip heavy cream and vanilla with beater, whisk electric mixer until soft peaks form and it becomes thick and creamy.

Sizzling Apple

1 apple
1 tsp lemon juice
1 tsp cinnamon
1 tbsp butter
1 cup heavy cream

Peel the apple and slice in to thin slices. Put apple slices in a skillet, add lemon juice, cinnamon and butter and cook on medium heat for 3-5 minutes or until apple is soft. Stir occasionally. Meanwhile whip heavy cream with beater, whisk electric mixer until soft peaks form and it becomes thick and creamy.

Put apples in a bowl and top with a dollop of whip cream. You may have extra whipped cream you can save and put in some decaf coffee.

German Chocolate Nests

Midway through making the filling for this recipe you may be looking side-ways into the pan and wondering, "Can this be right?!" Yes, yes it is. No worries. Keep your eyes on the prize and know that, although really funny looking during the cooking process, this dessert will be delicious. And look delicious, too, when all is said and done.

For Nests:
1/4 cup cocoa powder
2 tbsp stevia
2 tbsp honey
2 1/2 cups unsweetened coconut
3 egg whites
1 tsp vanilla extract or 1 drop essential oil

Preheat oven to 325 F. Line cookie sheet with Parchment paper. Mix all ingredients together. With wet hands, form mixture into 1-inch balls, then use fingers to form each ball into a "nest". Place on prepared cookie sheet. Bake for 16 minute, rotating pan half-way through.

For Filling:
3/4 cup unsweetened coconut, toasted
1/2 cup pecans, chopped and toasted
1/2 cup almond milk
1/4 cup heavy cream
1 tbsp chia seeds
1 tbsp honey

1 tbsp stevia
2 tbsp coconut oil
1 tsp vanilla extract or 1 drop essential oil
2 eggs, beaten

Combine almond milk, heavy cream and chia seeds in a saucepan (no heat yet) and let sit for 15-20 minutes until thickened. Then place pan on low-medium heat and whisk in remaining ingredients. Stir constantly while cooking for several minutes, until mixture thickens and reaches 140 degrees. Remove from heat and let cool to room temp. Stir in toasted coconut and toasted pecans. Fill each baked "nest" with filling. Serve as is or top with additional toasted coconut or chocolate drizzle.

For Topping (if Desired):
1/4 cup toasted unsweetened coconut
Drizzle dark chocolate, melted

Pumpkin Pie Raw

2 cups pecans (or walnuts)
1 1/2 cups pitted dates, soaked for 1 hour
Pinch of sea salt
1 15-oz can natural pumpkin puree
2 tsp ground cinnamon
1 tsp ground ginger
1 tsp grated nutmeg
1/2 tsp allspice
1/2 cup coconut oil, melted
1/4 tsp vanilla powder
1/4 cup almond milk or water (optional)

For the crust, simply add the pecans, 1/2 cup of the soaked dates, and a pinch of salt to the food processor and blend until sticking together into a dough-like consistency. Transfer to a pie or quiche plate, and press down with your hands.

For the filling, blend all the rest of the ingredients for a few minutes until completely smooth and creamy. If the consistency isn't smooth enough, add some almond milk or water. This may take longer than you think; be patient! Pour the filling onto the crust, cover with cling film and refrigerate for at least an hour (overnight is best).

Berry Cake

2 tbsp unsalted butter
1 1/2 cups raspberries, strawberries, blackberries, or blueberries
5 large eggs, separated
1/2 tsp cinnamon

Preheat over to 400 F. Heat butter in a skillet over medium heat and add berries (your choice of berries, or combination of berries listed above). Simmer until liquefied. While berries are cooking, in a separate bowl mix the yokes with a fork and add cinnamon. Separately mix the egg whites with a mixer until fluffy. Gently mix in the yoke mix with the egg whites mix and pour over the berry mixture. Leave on stove for 2 minutes on low heat and then place in oven for 10 minutes. Upon removing the cake from the oven, flip the berry cake over so the berry side is on top. Enjoy this sweet dish.

Homemade Chocolate

4 ounces dark chocolate
2 cups coconut oil
1 tsp salt

Put dark chocolate in a microwaveable bowl and cook on high for 30 seconds and stir until all chocolate is melted. Add coconut oil to bowl and stir. Put back in microwave for 30 seconds and then stir. Repeat until chocolate is melted. Line a baking sheet with parchment paper and then pour chocolate mixture on the prepared sheet. Sprinkle with salt and put in fit in the freezer for 15 minutes or until solid. Cut chocolate into squares and put back in to freezer to store.

Applesauce and Granola

4 lbs. apples, cut into small chunks
3 tsp cinnamon
3 tsp cardamom
2 cups strong brewed earl grey or lavender tea
1 tbsp lemon juice
Pumpkin Granola (recipe in desserts)

Combine apples, cinnamon, cardamom, tea and lemon juice in a crockpot and cook for 4 hours. Serve with granola on top.

Pumpkin Muffins

1/2 cup coconut flour
1 1/2 tsp cinnamon
1/2 tsp nutmeg
2 tsp pumpkin pie spice
1/2 tsp baking soda
1/2 tsp salt
1-15 oz can of pumpkin
6 eggs, beaten
4 tbsp coconut oil
1/3 cup honey
1 tsp vanilla extract or 1 drop essential oil
3/4 cup dark chocolate chips

Preheat oven to 400 F, grease muffin pan well or line with muffin liners. Combine coconut flour, baking soda, salt and spices in a small bowl. Blend well and set aside. Mix eggs and pumpkin in a medium bowl . Add melted coconut oil, honey and vanilla and mix well. Then add flour mixture to pumpkin mixture and blend well with a whisk just until the lumps are all gone. Stir in chocolate chips. Spoon the mixture into the muffin cups to 2/3 full. Bake for 18-20 minutes, until golden brown on top and inserted tooth-pick comes out clean. Cool on a rack and serve.

Almond Butter Cookies

1 egg
1 tsp vanilla extract or 1 drop essential oil
1 tsp almond extract
1/3 cup xylitol
15 drops stevia liquid
1 cup almond butter, unsalted
1/4 tsp sea salt

Preheat oven to 350 F. Using an electronic mixer or food processor, beat together egg, vanilla and almond extract, salt, stevia and xylitol. After well mixed, add in almond butter and mix well. Form balls and place 1 inch apart on parchment paper lined baking sheet. Flatten with fork to make crisscross design. Bake 10-12 minutes. Remove cookies from oven but do not touch until they are completely cooled (cookies will fall apart if you touch too soon). Remove from parchment paper and place in a airtight container and store in fridge. You can make a double batch and freeze too.

Beverages

Coffee smoothie

1 packet of instant decaf or regular coffee
1 cup ice
1 cup unsweetened almond milk
1 scoop protein powder (optional)

Blend all ingredients in a blender until smooth and enjoy.

Banana Smoothie

1 banana
1 cup unsweetened almond milk
1 egg
1 pinch of cinnamon

Blend all ingredients in a blender until smooth and enjoy.

Kale Smoothie

1 cup firmly packed kale
1 cup fresh or frozen berries (strawberries, blackberries, or
    blueberries)
1 cup Greek yogurt
1 cup ice

Blend all ingredients in a blender until smooth and enjoy.

Pumpkin Coffee Creamer

1 cup heavy cream

2 tsp vanilla extract

3 tsp pumpkin pie spice

1/4 cup pumpkin puree

Blend all ingredients together by stirring or shaking. Serve with coffee

Egg Nog Coffee Creamer

1 cup heavy cream

2 tsp vanilla extract

1 tsp cinnamon

1 tsp nutmeg

3 drops clove essential oil or 1 tsp ground glove

Blend all ingredients together by stirring or shaking. Serve with coffee.

Peppermint Mocha Coffee Creamer

1 cup heavy cream
2 tbsp cocoa powder
1 tsp peppermint extract or 6-8 drops peppermint essential oil
1/4 cup hot water

Mix the cocoa powder with the hot water and shake or stir until well blended and no longer lumpy. Add all other ingredients and shake lightly or stir. Serve with coffee.

Mint Iced Tea

4 Tea Bags (black tea recommended)
1 bunch of mint

Place warm filtered water in a pitcher. Steep bags in water at room temperature until tea is desired strength. Mash mint in pitcher. Once tea is desired strength you can refrigerate for at least an hour and then serve. Keep mint in pitcher until tea is gone.

Basil Lemon Spritzer

1 tbsp water
10 blackberries
Juice from 1 lemon
4 fresh basil leaves
1 cup club soda

Cut the blackberries into small pieces, add all ingredients to shaker, cover tightly and shake until blended. Strain over glass with ice and enjoy.

Made in the USA
San Bernardino, CA
07 September 2017

Simply YEAST Free

Main Courses, Desserts, and MORE....

Katy Langkamp & Kindsey Pentecost Neeson

Photographs by Brittany Ykema

Hummingbird Facts

Hello, Dear Readers!

Did you know that there are hummingbirds hidden in the illustrations of this book? How many can you find?

The hummingbird's hum comes from the sound of their wings flapping.

Hummingbirds live in North and South America. Many species migrate to warm climates each winter, though some live year-round in places where the climate is mild.

Mother hummingbirds build tiny nests shaped like cones out of twigs and leaves.

Hummingbirds drink nectar from flowers and eat small insects. They will also drink sugar water from feeders.

Hummingbirds have great vision and can see bright colors especially well. They often go to red, orange, and yellow flowers to find the best nectar.

Hummingbirds' wings beat so fast that they cannot be seen by the human eye!